Moon Aft

Daily Meditations Using the
Moon Phase to Focus Your Energy

Eileen Troemel

Moon Affirmations:
Daily Meditations Using the Moon Phase to Focus Your Energy

Eileen Troemel

Illustrations by

TJ Jahns

Moon Affirmations Daily Meditations Using the Moon Phase to Focus Your Energy

© 2014 by Eileen Troemel

Published by Stone Publishing
 A division of Stone Enterprising

Cover Photo by Suzanne Inez Jaillet-Isham

Other books by this author:
Secret Past

Acknowledgements:

Thank you to my husband Ken and my daughters who support me. Thank you to Laura who lay on the ground staring at the stars with me at the inception of the book. Thank you to Suzanne for creative assistance with the cover. Without these and others, this book would never have gotten off the ground. Thank you to TJ for creating lovely images to enhance the meditations and affirmations.

Table of Contents

Introduction:
For the Beginner:
Chapter 1: New Moon
    Beginnings
    Choice1
    Reaching for the Stars
Chapter 2: First Crescent
    Veils
    Young
    My Veil
Chapter 3: First Quarter
    Each Step
    Heavenly Games
    I Am a Goddess (God)
Chapter 4: Gibbous Moon
    Nature's Gifts
    Nurturer
    I Go Within
Chapter 5: Full Moon
    Full Moon
    Balance
    Moon of Delight
Chapter 6: Disseminating Moon
    Life Cycles
    Letting go
    Pools of Order and Chaos
Chapter 7: Last Quarter
    Release
    Celestial Guidance
    Walls
Chapter 8: Balsamic Moon
    Turning Wheel
    Composting
    Cocoon

Chapter 9: Dark Moon
    Cauldron of Life
    Cosmic Cauldron
    Energy
    Possibilities
Resources
A Note from the Author
About the Author
About the Artist

Introduction:

Usually you are so busy giving your all to others you forget about yourself. Putting yourself first is usually the last thing you do. Yet at some point, usually on the verge of exhaustion, you begin to think that maybe you need to make time for you. By taking care of yourself first, you are better able to keep giving it all to those important people in your life.

When you look for your stress relief activity, there are many options. Maybe it's a weekend away at a spa meant to refresh and rejuvenate your spirit. Maybe it's taking an hour in the tub with a good book. Let's get real. Between kids, lovers, pets, work, housework, and whatever else there is in your already too full life when do you get even 15 minutes to yourself?

Moon Affirmations is meant to give you those 15 minutes (and maybe a bit more) to help you feel better about yourself by focusing your energy on YOU. These affirmations tap into the energy of the ever changing moon to help you deal with whatever is most needed at that moment. Keeping in mind your already crowded schedule, each night has a short affirmation poem and meditation activity focusing on the energy of the moon phase. The meditations are meant to take very little time but still delve deeply into your inner self to bring you insight.

Each moon phase lasts slightly longer than three days with the full cycle of the moon lasting about 29.5 days. This book has three meditations per phase with one extra meditation to help fill in the added time per phase. The phases of the moon represent different energy. For instance, the new moon represents rebirth while a waning moon represents letting go. These energies can be used to focus meditations. The journey can start at any time during the moon phases, just turn to the appropriate page and start down the path.

The book begins with the new moon energy; the affirmations take you through a birth of self discovery to reawaken your awareness of who you are and what you want to do. Just as the new moon is dark and unrevealing, many of your aspects may be hidden. These affirmations help you look at these aspects of self and discover how they make up your core.

As the nights go by and the moon's phase shifts to the first crescent, the young energy of the moon phase infuses the affirmations and the meditations with childlike enthusiasm. You are encouraged to play and be silly to match the youthfulness of the phase.

The first quarter you are beginning to find your rhythm and take your first steps just as a toddler would. This quarter is to help you with those first steps in new projects and new beginnings while still embracing the playfulness of the young. Embracing childlike behavior helps you to relieve stress and reconnect to your dreams.

The gibbous moon brings a gathering of energy, a filling of your inner talents and joys. You discover who you are. You tap into the energy of the young adult, and rediscover the confidence that you can do or be anything.

By the full moon you are full of your own power and your own strengths. You are meant to share these gifts. These affirmations are about giving birth to a more confident you and sharing the energy of birth with all.

As the moon begins to fade from full to disseminating, so does your energy shift from sending out positive and loving energy to turn away from the public self to look within. It is about taking a longer look at who you are. The light still shines on you from the moon and into your soul but now is a good time to see for yourself what is there.

When you look within you are likely to find things you don't want or need any longer. The last quarter is the time to start shedding these things. Let go of the old so you can embrace a new and better you. This is the phase where you recognize any changes you need to make.

As the moon shifts into the balsamic phase, it is time to wash away the old habits to make room for the better and stronger you. This phase is meant to help you shed the things that don't work for you. It is time to harvest all you have learned before you move forward.

The dark moon shifts you from fixing aspects of yourself to settling into how you are. You have worked hard over the last month to give birth to a new you. With the dark moon, you should let things settle into a new picture because in just a few days you will be giving birth again to a new you. Take this time to stir the inner parts of you and see how they fit with all the insight of the previous work

The last meditation is about all the possibilities. The moon takes 29.5 days to work through her cycle and while there are three meditations per phase, each phase is a bit more than three days. Perhaps before you begin your journey through the moon's phases, start with this meditation to see what options you discover. When done with your journey through the moon's phases do it again to see what changed.

As you do meditations, you will be travelling into territory previously unexplored. These journeys can create a heady almost intoxicated feeling. When you are done with a meditation it is advisable to ground yourself. Grounding is the process of bringing your awareness back to your physical body. It means to become aware of being within your own body. Give yourself time to reacquaint your mental self with your physical self. There are many ways to ground yourself and during some of the meditations it is explicitly stated to do this. Whether it is stated or not, you should always take the time to ground yourself after meditating.

The purpose of this book is to give a positive lift to your life, to help you feel better about yourself. The format is one I think will fit into most lives as it isn't too time consuming nor does it require a great deal of technique. It is meant to be simple but to offer deep thought provoking results.

"See how nature - trees, flowers, grass - grows in silence; see the stars, the moon and the sun, how they move in silence...we need silence to be able to touch souls." Mother Theresa of Calcutta.

For the Beginner:

Begin each meditation by getting in a comfortable position. This does not have to be sitting with legs crossed and hands on knees. It can be sitting in a recliner, laying on the floor, or any other position you are comfortable. The point is to be physically comfortable so you can let go of your physical body and focus on your spiritual energy.

Relax and take a deep breath. For several minutes just focus on your breathing. Have a slow deep breath in. Hold it for a moment. Release it slowly and deliberately. As you breathe you will feel yourself relax. This will not instantly send you to a meditative state. Hear the world around you. Hear the dog snuffling, the cat scratching on her post. Acknowledge all the noises, identify them and let them go. They should become like white noise in the background.

Feel your world around you. As you hear noises incorporate this into your meditation. Each meditation should begin like this. When you have reached a relaxed state, go into the guided meditation. Reaching a relaxed state may take you several attempts. Don't be surprised if you find yourself making a mental to-do list or dozing off. The idea is to allow your mind to recognize what is going on and bring it back to the meditative state.

You can record the guided meditation. Make sure to add in pauses. Or you can have someone read it to you. Another option is to memorize the meditation; this may be difficult but if you hold the general ideas in your mind as you meditate it will help you take the journey you seek.

To ground yourself you can touch the ground or furniture. Slowly move and stretch, focus on the act of moving. Don't rush up and out of the meditation. Give your mind and spirit time to reconnect with your body. If after these types of grounding activities you still feel disconnected then eat some earthy types of food like bread or root vegetable including potatoes or carrots. Because these items come from the earth they help to bring your awareness back to the physical world.

It's important to remember that sometimes meditation will take you were you need to go rather than where you intended to go. As you're doing these meditations if you find yourself in a different place than described, go where the energy takes you. Our spirit moves us where we need to be, if you just trust yourself.

Chapter 1: New Moon

The new moon phase represents new beginnings. The start of everything whether it is new projects, new job, new love, new phase in life or new perspective. The moon's face is in silhouette as the moon lies between the sun and earth. This phase is not about seeing but about all the other senses including your own intuition.

The natural darkness of the nights lends itself to an opportunity to use your other senses. Listen to your own heart beating, the wind in the trees, the night sounds around you and discover how they make you feel.

As a new love makes you giddy, the new moon can bring the same excitement. You could embark on a new job, start a new relationship (even if it is with yourself), or anything else. The opportunities are endless and bound only by your imagination.

These three meditations take you through beginnings, choices and dreams.

Night 1: The dark new moon has no light to lead you. It is a time of birth and beginnings. Repeat this chant while sitting in the dark:

Beginnings

I am reborn,
I am vulnerable,
I am beginning,

I seek a path
I seek wisdom
I seek knowledge

Sprinkles of diamonds
Across the velvety sky
Each is a dream
Waiting to be plucked
To bring great satisfaction
For the one
Courageous enough
To reach the greatest of heights.

Each night you meditate, take the time to relax, be comfortable, and prepare yourself as described in the For Beginners section.

Sit in the dark. Listen to the sounds around you. Identify each sound. Make the sound a part of the background web in your life. Breathe in deeply, slowly release the breath. Continue slowly breathing until each sound becomes like your breath; an automatic part of your being. Visualize yourself at the center of a circle. Leading away from the center are many paths. Slowly turn around seeing each path leading away. As you turn, one path may draw you, look down the path. What do you see? Take time to complete the circle. There may be more than one path which draws you, determine which has the strongest pull. This is a night to see the options available to you. Take time to consider each possible path. It is the beginning of birthing a new life for you.

When you are through, ground and balance yourself. Allow your awareness to return to where you sit. Become aware of the ground or furniture you are sitting on and your physical surroundings. Bring your awareness back to your physical body. As you become more aware, rest your hands on the ground and allow yourself to feel your physical surroundings. This will help bring your energy and awareness back to a centered and balanced place.

When you meditate it is very important to bring your center back to your physical being. Ground yourself in one of the ways suggested in the For Beginners section.

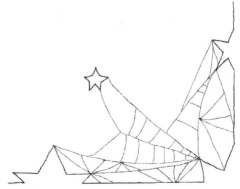

Night 2: The energy of the moon works to begin a new cycle of growth. It is a time to choose which path you wish to follow for this moon cycle. To set the mood read and repeat the following:

Choice

I am choosing
I am learning
I am seeking

Before me is a path
Before me is a future
Before me is a dream

Soaring through the air
I climb higher and higher
Stretching my limits
Pushing my boundaries
Risking it all
To begin my journey

Each night you meditate, take the time to relax, be comfortable, and prepare yourself as described in the For Beginners section.

Relax and settle into a safe and calm place to explore your inner paths. Sit in the dark and listen to your surroundings.

Center and breathe, putting all the noises into the web. When you are calm, centered and balanced, go to the circle. See the paths which draw you. They glow slightly. Each path may have a symbol or image. There may be a texture you feel under your feet or in your hands. You may smell something familiar or taste something different from the other paths. Step onto the path which draws you the most and creates the strongest reaction in you. Stand at the beginning. Note your reaction and which sense it comes through. How does it make you feel? Step back into the center of the circle. Try each path. The first steps of birth are taken in identifying the path you should follow. Take time to consider each option.

When you are through ground and balance yourself. Allow yourself to feel your physical body and sense your surroundings. Listen for the sounds in your home or in nature. Smell the candle burning or the air around you. Feel the hardness of the earth beneath you or the solid furniture you sit on.

When you meditate it is very important to bring your center back to your physical being. Ground yourself in one of the ways suggested in the For Beginners section.

Night 3: The last night of the new moon brings a decision as to which path to follow. You may feel giddy with excitement and a touch of fear for stepping into the unknown. Embrace this excitement but don't allow it to draw you recklessly down a path. To focus your energy repeat this:

Reaching for the Stars

I choose to be strong
I choose to learn
I choose my direction

I reach for my dream
I reach for my inner power
I reach for my new destination

Standing on a precipice
The wind pushes me higher
I'm flying to the stars
Pulling from them
The joy of striving
The pride of accomplishment
The excitement of a new beginning

Each night you meditate, take the time to relax, be comfortable, and prepare yourself as described in the For Beginners section.

Relax and release the stresses of the day. Breathe deeply and relax into a meditative state. See yourself at the center of a circle. If you have done the previous two nights revisit the circle in your mind. See the path you had chosen and step onto the one you travel on tonight. Look forward and see what lies along this path. See the twists and turns, peaks and valleys. Follow the path, noting any reaction in any of your senses. Listen for any messages. Don't rush. Take in all that surrounds you. The path will bring you to a hill, at the top of the hill there is a bench. Sit on this bench and take note of how the path travels down the hill and where it leads. Feel what the bench is made of. Use all of your senses to familiarize yourself with the bench. See sign posts along the way giving you messages of encouragement and direction. The birth has happened. You may feel nervous or afraid. Birth and change are sometimes very difficult. Sit on the bench to allow yourself time to adjust.

When you've accepted the path and become comfortable with the birth, come back to your physical self. Ground and balance yourself. Bring your senses back to your physical surroundings and take a few deep slow breaths as you bring your consciousness back to your body.

When you meditate it is very important to bring your center back to your physical being. Ground yourself in one of the ways suggested in the For Beginners section.

Chapter 2: First Crescent

With the first crescent moon, light returns to the night sky. This phase goes from the first appearance of the moon and ends before the moon is half illuminated. You receive a glimmer to help you see the path you seek.

The first blush is off the new project you've started. You can start to see the path you've chosen and you begin the first tentative steps on the road. The giddiness of the new love has settled into an excitement but a realization that there will be work involved.

A sliver of light has illuminated the night sky and your inner journey. The first initial steps of the journey begin with tentative steps towards your goal.

The phase is about being new and gaining confidence in yourself as you start the journey. It is about building on your own feelings of self worth and assurance to move forward.

As the light grows, so does your faith in your own abilities. These meditations help you begin to reveal yourself to you and to the world.

Night 4: The first crescent moon is peeking out from the veil of the new moon. She begins by showing just a glimmer of herself. To tap into the energy repeat the following:

Veils

Tonight I show,
My eyes to the world.
I peek from behind,
A veil of darkness.
To offer a glimpse of wisdom,
For the first tentative steps,
On a new journey.
Look up to see my sliver,
Of illumination.
Look within,
To find your own.

Each night you meditate, take the time to relax, be comfortable, and prepare yourself as described in the For Beginners section.

Light a single candle, play music, something playful and sassy. Lie on the floor covered with a blanket. As the music starts, let your fingers or toes tap. Flow with the music, play peek-a-boo with the light. Move with the music like a small child dances. Get up and dance. Embrace the silliness of it. Use the blanket to hide and reveal yourself while you dance.

Even if you have limited mobility, dance while you sit in a chair or as you lie in bed. Embrace the excitement and joy of a new beginning. This moving meditation allows you to rejoice in the new beginning which has started. Let your inhibitions go. Don't be afraid to look silly, just do it and enjoy.

When you meditate it is very important to bring your center back to your physical being. Ground yourself in one of the ways suggested in the For Beginners section.

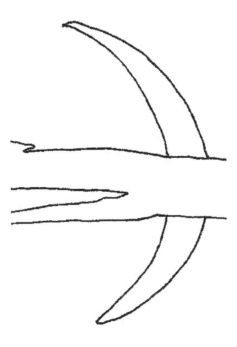

Night 5: The second night of the first crescent is here. Allow yourself to feel young and renewed. Rebirth gives way to a new you. Embrace your inner child. Repeat this as you meditate:

Young

I am young,
In mind, body, and spirit.
I am playful,
Because it helps balance life.
I am fearful,
But excited to begin a new quest.
I am enthusiastic,
To learn and grow with each experience.
I am daring,
Exploring new uncharted avenues.
I am adventurous,
Climbing the mountain just to see.

Each night you meditate, take the time to relax, be comfortable, and prepare yourself as described in the For Beginners section.

Settle down to meditate, stilling your mind and body. Release the stress of the day, breathe deeply and exhale away the tension in your mind, body, and spirit.

Visualize yourself on a bench at the top of the hill. Look behind you; see the rough road and steep incline. Acknowledge the accomplishment, give a holler of exultation. See the path ahead of you as an adventure and begin down the hill.

Stop at all the signs and symbols. Use the pale light of the crescent moon to read the signs. Touch them. Use all your senses; smell the wind blowing across the landscape or the flowers at your feet. Feel the texture of the path.

As you start up the next incline, feel the pull in your legs. Your body struggles. Your inner mind does the same. At the top rest and reflect. Is there a well with a bucket of cold water? Splash some on your face and refresh yourself. Look back at the path, see your accomplishment and understand the work you have done.

Consider what this path symbolizes? What are the messages you received from your sign posts? Take time to consider the journey so far.

When you're through contemplating, ground and balance yourself as you return to the physical world.

When you meditate it is very important to bring your center back to your physical being. Ground yourself in one of the ways suggested in the For Beginners section.

Night 6: The moon grows bigger with each night; just as your awareness grows while traversing your inner landscape. Change often brings resistance. Accept it as part of the journey but don't allow it to stop you from further self discovery. Repeat this as you settle into meditation:

My Veil

My veil I've dropped,
As I run through a field of tall grass
Laughing with the trees,
Stars shine bright twinkling with suppressed giggles
At the feeble attempts
Of fireflies to mimic their glow.

My veil I've dropped
In my excitement for the new journeys
I illuminate to help
Mortals see their way
With a silvery moonbeam
Blessing their quest
Through space and time
To grow and change.

Each night you meditate, take the time to relax, be comfortable, and prepare yourself as described in the For Beginners section.

If it is warm enough, take a blanket outside and stare up at the night sky. Can you see the crescent moon? If you can, stare at her till you see nothing else, become the moon. (If the moon is hidden by trees or clouds select a star.) Feel the gentle warmth of her light surround you. See the soft light push back the darkness surrounding it.

Feel the rapture the moon has in being reborn. Let the celestial being enfold you. This is meant to help you adjust to the changes you are experiencing. Take this night to embrace the phase of the moon and your phase of life.

Note: if you are unable to go outside to do this exercise you can do it inside with visualization. If you have a hard time visualizing the moon, find or draw a picture of it and stare at it while you go into a meditative state.

When you meditate it is very important to bring your center back to your physical being. Ground yourself in one of the ways suggested in the For Beginners section.

Chapter 3: First Quarter

In the first quarter, the moon shines with half her face illuminated. The moon phase is gaining strength and energy as more light is revealed. The energy renews your confidence and sheds light on these moments in your life. The light shines on you and your path. The confidence gained is grasped with both hands as you take control of your dreams and hopes.

The building of the light gives you confidence to critique your habits and life. Is there a better way? If you don't know find out by exploring possibilities. The light of the moon illuminates the options available.

These meditations help you think outside your comfort zone for alternatives to what is not working for you. They help you reach for the stars and embrace change.

Night 7: As the moon grows, you may find yourself with more energy and more creative forces. Chant this while settling into a meditative mood:

Each Step

Each step I take
Moves me further
Along my road
To discovery

Each step I take
Teaches me more
About my inner self
And my path

Each step I take
Enables me to
See old pains
From a new perspective

Each step I take
Builds me a better
Inner temple where
I learn to love myself

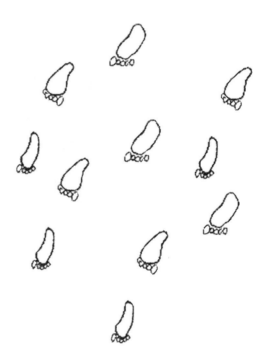

Each night you meditate, take the time to relax, be comfortable, and prepare yourself as described in the For Beginners section.

Get a set of building blocks. Play with them. Build different structures. Take some time and have fun building up and crashing the structures down. Enjoy and laugh at your own playfulness.

When you have finished playing with the blocks, take a single block and name it for a moral belief, characteristic or a life forming experience. Think of the moments which stand out in your life, both positive and negative. Place the block in the foundation of your temple. Keep adding and naming blocks until you have built your temple. Use post-its or crayons to write or draw a symbol on the block.

If possible leave your temple up for display. If you learn more from drawing, you can also draw your temple using symbols for each of your beliefs. Or if you are artistically challenged, look through magazines and newspapers for symbols of your beliefs and create a collage.

When you meditate it is very important to bring your center back to your physical being. Ground yourself in one of the ways suggested in the For Beginners section.

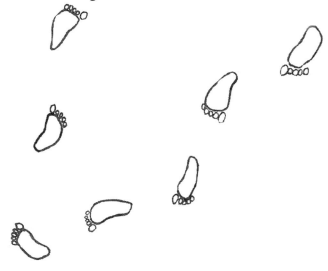

Night 8: The first quarter is about building yourself up by recognizing your true self. It is a time to find new solutions to old problems which you have now seen from a new perspective. This is the moon phase where the physical work needs to be done. Begin meditation with the following:

Heavenly Games

Skipping across Orion
Landing in the curve
Of the crescent moon
Laughing as I play
Across the night sky

Bathing in the big dipper
Blowing bubbles at Ursa Major
Dive off the handle
To land with a giggle
In the gentle curve

Mother moon cradles me
Close to her heart
She catches me before I fall
As I scamper and play
Among the stars

Each night you meditate, take the time to relax, be comfortable, and prepare yourself as described in the For Beginners section.

If you are able, go out under the first quarter moon. Gaze up at the stars, picking out the constellations you know. Depending on your location and the time of year, you will see different constellations in the sky. As you find the constellations, play with the stars – jump, hopscotch or skip rope. Then let your eyes wander back to the moon. Rest and absorb her youthful energy.

As you rest in the moon, think of the lessons your parents, grandparents and other elders taught you. How many of those lessons are incorporated into your foundation of beliefs? What lessons would you pass on to others?

Don't dwell, rest for a few moments and determine one or two basic beliefs then move back to the constellations for some light hearted fun.

Repeat this process until you can think of no more fundamental beliefs. Make sure you end the session with some fun jumping from star to star.

When you meditate it is very important to bring your center back to your physical being. Ground yourself in one of the ways suggested in the For Beginners section.

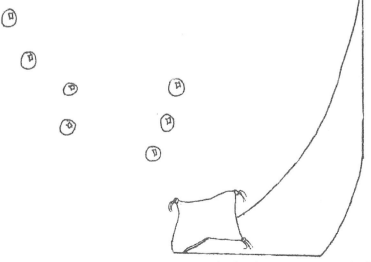

Night 9: The first quarter is about questioning the status quo. In questioning why you do something. If and the answer is because it has always been done this way, it may be time to change your ways. Demand change, even if it is difficult.

This affirmation is meant to help you tap into the divine energy. Choose the term you are most comfortable with and use this empowering chant to find inner strength.

I Am a Goddess (God)

I am a builder
Growing from a foundation
Of positive and nurturing beliefs

I am a creator
Developing my inner self
From star dust and moonbeams

I am an artist
Painting a masterpiece
With my dreams and desires

I am a Goddess (God)
Directing my destiny
With my thoughts and deeds

Each night you meditate, take the time to relax, be comfortable, and prepare yourself as described in the For Beginners section.

If your blocks are still set up as your temple, sit down with them. Look at your building. If you took out one block would the whole thing tumble down? How many blocks would it take for the structure to fall?

Now think on your beliefs which the blocks represent? What would happen to your inner temple if one of your beliefs were to change drastically? Think of how your beliefs change and grow as you do. Should your beliefs be pliable or rigid? Which beliefs are finite and haven't changed over time? Which ones have changed? Determine how stable your inner temple is.

If you created a collage or drawing to represent your temple, gaze at that and determine how it would be different if you had chosen a different symbol for one of your beliefs. How would it be different if you used a different color? Look over your foundations and see how they could be changed and forged into something new and better.

When you meditate it is very important to bring your center back to your physical being. Ground yourself in one of the ways suggested in the For Beginners section.

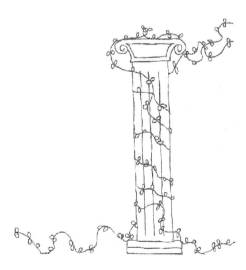

Chapter 4: Gibbous Moon

Edging towards the full moon, the gibbous moon is more than half illuminated but not quite full. This is the calm before the full moon.

As the light grows even brighter in the night your confidence grows. You become comfortable with where you are and the work you are doing on yourself. Perhaps you have faced some difficulties which need time to heal. Take the time; let the light of the moon fill you with peace and calm.

The journey within can be rough and rocky. Let the light from this moon soothe the rough edges from your soul. Change is inevitable but it can also be difficult. Allow yourself this time to adjust. Embrace the light from the moon to fill up all the empty places in you. Allow yourself joy in who you are.

These meditations help you cope with the choices you have made by filling you with healing energy.

Night 10: Energy is gathering within and preparing to be sent out. As you settle to mediation chant the following to assist in setting the mood:

Nature's Gifts

I am the wind
Whispering through the trees
Hinting of seasons past
And those yet to come

I bring cooling fresh air
On a sweltering summer day
To cool fevered minds
And gift creative thoughts

I rush across the landscape
Carrying storm clouds
And turmoil away
Leaving change and rebirth in my wake

Each night you meditate, take the time to relax, be comfortable, and prepare yourself as described in the For Beginners section.

The moon will rise just before sunset. If possible watch it rise. Feel the breeze on your face, lifting your hair. Close your eyes and breathe in deeply. Smell the freshness of the air. Allow the breeze to blow away the cobwebs of the day. In your mind's eye see all the stressful things from your day fluttering out behind you like a fall leaf riding the breeze.

When the stresses have cleared, take another slow deep breath. Let your mind quiet, stare at the moon and let her fill you up. Let the soft light flood into your being to soothe away any remaining stresses. Fill yourself with the positive healing energy of the gibbous moon.

When you meditate it is very important to bring your center back to your physical being. Ground yourself in one of the ways suggested in the For Beginners section.

Night 11: With the gibbous moon, explore new ways of doing things. Embrace the calm outlook and look for ways to improve yourself and your world. Write your own affirmation if you feel able. Use I am statements of power. If you don't want to write your own, use the one below:

Nurturer

I am a nurturer
I am a caretaker
I am a healer

I begin with myself
I begin with my soul
I begin with my body

I send energy to my family
I send energy to my friends
I send energy to the world

I am a nurturer
I am a caretaker
I am a healer

Each night you meditate, take the time to relax, be comfortable, and prepare yourself as described in the For Beginners section.

If possible go out under the moon to do this. If not possible, visualize yourself standing in a clearing. The moon is nearly full and hanging overhead lighting the meadow. See yourself standing under the moon.

See a moon beam come down to surround you with gentle, soft, healing light. Let it fill you up and carry away your stresses and strains. As calm spreads, you feel the healing of the moonbeam wash over you like a soothing summer shower.

When you feel centered and balanced, direct the moonbeam's energy into your hands. Shape it into a small ball and let it grow. Say quietly the names of the people you want to send positive energy to. Don't forget to start with yourself. With each name the ball gets larger.

When you can no longer hold the ball, throw it high in the air. See it blossom and scatter like fireworks. As the sparkling glittery lights go out, know the positive energy went to those you named and any others in need.

Make sure you ground and center after doing this healing exercise.

When you meditate it is very important to bring your center back to your physical being. Ground yourself in one of the ways suggested in the For Beginners section.

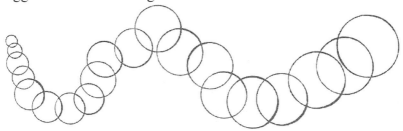

Night 12: As the gibbous moon grows to nearly full, feel the power of your own conviction and ability. You are able to heal your soul by embracing your own power. You have stood in a moonbeam and embraced the healing nature of the moon.

Returning to the inner journey use this meditative chant to bring the focus back to your own path:

I Go Within

I go within,
Seeking my path,
Looking backwards,
I find the crossroads,
Which brought me here.

I go within,
Seeing the moments,
Both joyful and sorrowful,
Which are the building blocks,
Of who I am.

I go within,
Forgiving myself for errors and slights,
Knowing these lessons,
Helped build my foundation,
To build my character

I go within,
Seeking my path forward,
Twists, turns, and mountains,
I will face as I go
With wisdom from lessons learned

Each night you meditate, take the time to relax, be comfortable, and prepare yourself as described in the For Beginners section.

After relaxing, see yourself on the hilltop bench. Behind you are all the moments of your life, some spotlighted and some in shadows.

A convoluted path lies before you, lighted by a nearly full moon. Take a moment to shed past resentments and heal old wounds – particularly those inflicted by you. See these falling from you in a shower of dust. Feel how light and at ease you are without the added burden of this dust.

Step forward on the path. Skip, run, or dance down the path letting the bright moonlight fill your heart and soul with positive loving energy. Notice any symbols, signs, or animals as you travel to the top of the next hill. Let all your senses awaken and be aware of your surroundings. Smell the night air, feel the texture of the path, hear the sounds of the environment around you.

Twirl around and shout for joy as the moon sends healing white light down upon you. Settle on the bench when you reach the top of the next hill. Look back at the things you've accomplished. Use the bright light from the moon to shed positive energy on all your experiences.

When you meditate it is very important to bring your center back to your physical being. Ground yourself in one of the ways suggested in the For Beginners section.

Chapter 5: Full Moon

The moon reveals her entire face to Earth. It is a time of balance in the cosmos between waxing and waning cycles.

There is a pause in the month while the full energy of the moon shines down. Like a teeter totter balanced, this is a time when you have taken in the growth and healing of the moon. You find a balance of energies in these three days.

With the full energy of the moon shining down, the path is illuminated and intentions become clear. All is revealed for your scrutiny. This moon phase is about the balance between taking in the new and releasing the old. This is when you have the clarity to examine all aspects of yourself.

These meditations assist you in that balance and the healing needed before you begin the process of letting go.

Night 13: The moon is pregnant with energy just waiting to be born and sent out into the world. The energy of this moon offers healing and love like a pregnant woman. Embrace this energy with this chant:

Full Moon

See my belly full and round
Nearly bursting with my children
Soon I'll birth them and name them
Creativity, love, healing, and more

The stars dim behind my bright light
Letting me shine forth to show the way
Fulfilling your dreams
With love and laughter

Send me your hopes and healing wishes
I'll shine down on those in need
Bringing them helpful energy and caring light
To illuminate their chosen path

See my belly full and round
Nearly bursting with my children
With joy I'll gift them to you
To use from this day forth

Each night you meditate, take the time to relax, be comfortable, and prepare yourself as described in the For Beginners section.

The moon rises roughly one hour after sunset. If you are able, go outside under the full moon. If not, visualize yourself standing by a lake with arms raised towards a full dazzling moon hanging low and reflected in the water.

See the light wash over you and across the landscape. Close your eyes and the gentle light shines through your lids. Recite the names of those you want to send energy to. Start with yourself. Chant the names repeatedly until the energy builds within. As the energy peaks, see light go from your hands to the moon and be spread out over the landscape like the beams from the full moon spreading out to those names and others in need. This light and energy is meant to reveal any sorrows and help heal them. It should help bring balance back to those who have areas in their lives that are out of balance.

Be sure to ground well after this. Eat, drink, dance or lay on the ground.

When you meditate it is very important to bring your center back to your physical being. Ground yourself in one of the ways suggested in the For Beginners section.

Night 14: The full moon is a time of balance. The sun and moon are in direct opposition to each other. Their energy is equal like twins sitting one on each side of a teeter totter.

Balance

Centered
Balance between waxing and waning
A brief moment in time
To reflect on what you have done
To look forward to what is to come
A pause of order between life's hectic chaos
To heal and gather encouraging energy and
To discard harmful aspects of self
An instant when everything is in order
Which will quickly slip away
Into the normal daily chaos.

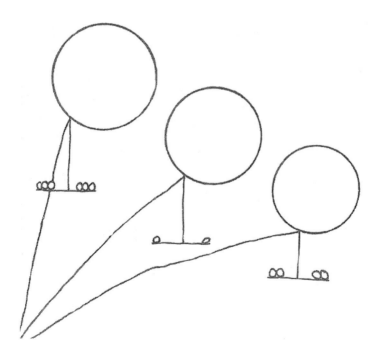

Each night you meditate, take the time to relax, be comfortable, and prepare yourself as described in the For Beginners section.

Relax and breathe deeply. Close your eyes. See yourself in the center of a teeter totter. On one end is accomplishment and completion; on the other is the prospect of new projects. When you look at the end with accomplishment, think of a time when you finished a big project. Think about how much satisfaction you felt with the completion. Allow the sense of accomplishment to wash over you like waves on a beach. Feel the joy at being done but also the sadness for an ending. With each ending in our life we grieve, whether for the loss of someone or something.

We must move on because each ending heralds a new start. Now turn to look at the other end where fresh starts are. Feel the excitement of starting a new project or new phase in life. See yourself reaching for the stars and you are just about to pluck one into your hand. Feel the joy and excitement of the anticipation.

New starts bring a giddiness of possibilities and a touch of fear for the unknown. Know that as you sit under the full moon in the center of the teeter totter you have a moment when you recognize and acknowledge both. In this moment you are in complete balance.

Allow your awareness to come back to yourself, bring with it the feeling of completion, accomplishment and the giddiness of new possibilities.

When you meditate it is very important to bring your center back to your physical being. Ground yourself in one of the ways suggested in the For Beginners section.

Night 15: The full moon slides towards waning. The balance starts to slide towards the releasing energy. Allow yourself to hold on for one more night to all your revelations.

Moon of Delight

Shining down with my soothing radiance
I am the moon curved and brilliant
Nestled in amongst the stars
I pull people from behind their inner bars
Gazing up they stammer with awe
I display my wonders before I withdraw

Sending creativity on shimmering moonbeams
I encourage all to reach for dreams
Showering down waves of healing
I answer calls of those appealing
Loving energy sprinkles out this night
I am the moon full of delight

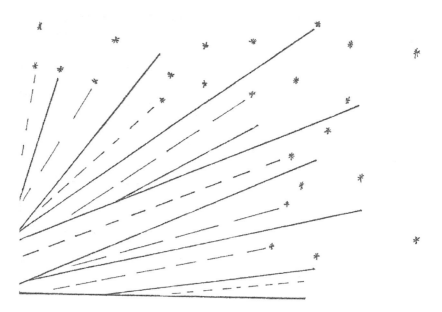

Each night you meditate, take the time to relax, be comfortable, and prepare yourself as described in the For Beginners section.

Under the light of the full moon become the moon. See the earth from far above. Look around to see the sparkling stars in the dark sky. Each star is a dream – reach out and pluck a handful. Look at the stars sparkling and glimmering in your hand. Feel the joy each dream will bring. Know the satisfaction of accomplishment upon attaining these dreams. Hold out your hand with the stars and gently blow them towards the earth. Watch as they shimmer while they fall.

After the last star has fallen, reach within your full moon belly and pull out a handful of moon beams. Bring these from your heart and infuse them with creativity, hope and encouragement. Pick the first moon beam and send it down. Watch as it covers part of the earth. Once it has faded, send out the next. Know that each one helps others grow. When you are done, twirl around in the night sky, thanking the stars and heavens. Then return to earth and look up at the moon you just were.

As you sent out the moonbeams, think about what else in your life needs to be sent out. Think about the dreams and stars you need to reach for. How will you accomplish them? What needs to change in your life to make it there?

Make sure you ground and balance after this exercise. As you come back to earth allow yourself to feel the joy and accomplishment of the dreams you have given and reached for within yourself. Remember that you are part of the earth and have these dreams and energy as well.

When you meditate it is very important to bring your center back to your physical being. Ground yourself in one of the ways suggested in the For Beginners section.

Chapter 6: Disseminating Moon

The disseminating moon is nearly full but not quite. It has faded from full but is more than half illuminated. This is the phase of the moon where you switch from sending your energy out into the world to looking within yourself to see what is working well and what needs changing.

You have brought in all the positive energy of the waxing moon. Now it is time to use that energy to discard the chaff in your life. What needs to change?

Even the most balanced and positive person can have problems letting go. At these times you have to accept that some chaos is bound to occur and you have to just ride through the bumpy rapids.

This phase is about small changes and preparing to let go of the negative aspects of your life. These meditations help you begin that process.

Night 16: The time to let go has come. This is difficult and should be done carefully. Recognize who you are now and acknowledge each stage in your life.

This affirmation has gender specific terms. Choose the one that fits you for the moment. This does not mean women must use the female terms, you decide what is right for each line:

Life Cycles

I am Goddess (God)
Both young and old
I am healer
At the birth of the universe
I am child
Learning wisdom from my elders
I am mother (father)
Nurturing those in need
I am crone (sage)
Teaching the young my insight
I am air
Bringing thoughts to those who will hear
I am fire
Sparking passion within open hearts
I am water
Overflowing with emotions
I am earth
Offering stability to those in need
I am spirit
Soaring through all

Each night you meditate, take the time to relax, be comfortable, and prepare yourself as described in the For Beginners section.

If you drum or have drumming music, repeat the chant very slowly, pausing after each statement. In your head see yourself as each statement. Take note of how it feels to be at each stage and in each situation. Listen for any messages at each stage. Look for any discomfort. Is there an element you are uncomfortable with? Is there a stage of life which draws you? Take note of these for later exploration. When you have gone through the entire array, feel the joy and knowledge you gain from each stage.

Each night you meditate, take the time to relax, be comfortable, and prepare yourself as described in the For Beginners section.

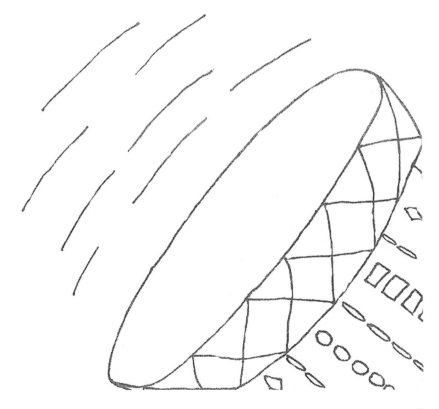

Night 17: As the moon wanes, it is time to harvest. Pluck all your revelations from the previous meditations. You have discovered things you no longer need. Perhaps it is time to clean closets both figuratively and literally.

This meditation will help you visualize the process of letting go:

Letting go

Little by little
Inch by inch
I let go

I shed unneeded
Habits and beliefs
I release old
Hurts and slights
I discard unwanted
Passions and baggage
I cast off unnecessary
Attachments and connections

Little by little
Inch by inch
I let go

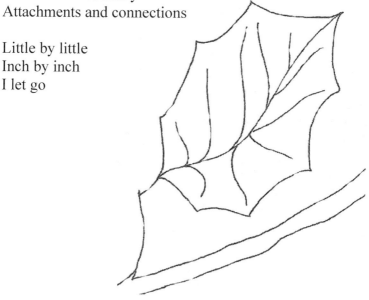

Each night you meditate, take the time to relax, be comfortable, and prepare yourself as described in the For Beginners section.

If you are able, go to your yard and lay under a large tree like a maple or oak. If you aren't able, then visualize yourself looking up at all the leaves clinging to the limbs. See the tree bloom in spring and the bud turn into a leaves. Clinging to the limb, the leaf survives through fierce spring and summer storms. Watch as neighboring leaves twitch and jump, falling away. Watch the leaves change colors to amber, ruby, and umber. Leaves fall and pile at the base. Wait as your leaf clings to the limb hoping for another hour or day of brilliance. The wind brushes through like a soft kiss goodnight and the leaf flutters free, floating on the breeze. Drifting lower and lower, buoyed by the playful autumn zephyr before finally settling on the ground.

The old order is gone; the leaf is no longer a part of the tree. Instead the leaf will decompose and become part of the soil. It will nourish the tree while it sleeps through the winter. Parts of the leaf will bud again in the spring to begin the journey again.

What part of you is that leaf? What do you need to release so it can decompose? Allow yourself to dwell here for a moment thinking of how life cycles.

You may cry or feel grieved by this process. Allow yourself to feel this.

Give yourself time to let go as you do this meditation. When your awareness comes back to you, don't rush up but allow yourself to rise slowly. Be gentle with yourself.

When you meditate it is very important to bring your center back to your physical being. Ground yourself in one of the ways suggested in the For Beginners section.

Night 18: The moon rises later and it is smaller each night. The energy is less frantic and more soothing as you learn to release.

Releasing can send you into a spiral of change, use this chant to assist with the change from turmoil to calm:

Pools of Order and Chaos

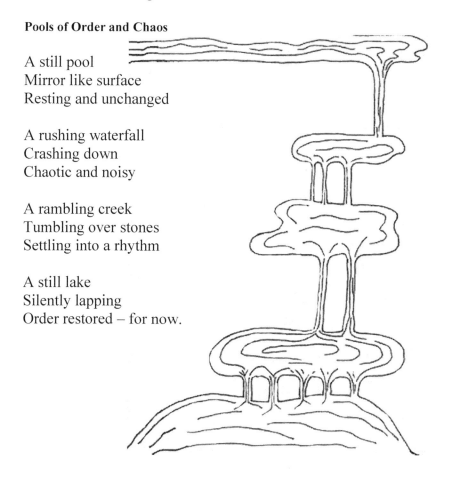

A still pool
Mirror like surface
Resting and unchanged

A rushing waterfall
Crashing down
Chaotic and noisy

A rambling creek
Tumbling over stones
Settling into a rhythm

A still lake
Silently lapping
Order restored – for now.

Each night you meditate, take the time to relax, be comfortable, and prepare yourself as described in the For Beginners section.

Underground water bubbles up out of the dark to be born into a cool quiet pool of water. Envision yourself as a drop of water bursting from the ground with the chaos of a birth.

Float into the pool, gentle and calm, leisurely traveling the length and breadth of the pool. Your world is at peace.

You become inexplicably drawn out of your calm, pulled like metal to a magnet. Rushing water thunders ahead and you have no choice. You tumble out of control, turning over and over, unsure of which way you are going. You fall endlessly. You feel helpless but amongst the chaos there is unity with those around you. They suffer the same chaotic fate. You plummet down, crashing into a whirlpool of turmoil.

You are thrown free. Life as a water drop slows. You pitch along the rocky bed sometimes out of control but more often it feels like you are riding a roller coaster up and down with laughter and a touch of fear.

At the end of the creek, you roll into a lake. You are no longer tottering along but gracefully rocking to and fro like a mother rocking her baby.

Identify the parallels between your journey as a water drop and your life. When have you floated as the water drop without direction or care? When have you been in turmoil like the waterfall? See the cycle of order turning to chaos and slowly turning back to order.

When you meditate it is very important to bring your center back to your physical being. Ground yourself in one of the ways suggested in the For Beginners section.

Chapter 7: Last Quarter

Once again the moon is showing only half her face. The focus remains within to assess your foundation of beliefs. The lack of light changes the focus from without to within.

The light decreases and you no longer see the path ahead but only the place you stand. On the journey within your discover parts of you which are no longer necessary. It is time to let them go. Release them out into the universe and let them be absorbed back into the universal consciousness.

Keep what is essential to you. Embrace the best parts of you. Like a spotlight, the smaller light allows you to focus in on these things.

These meditations help you see who you are and the walls you create to protect yourself. They help you determine what aspects of self you need to keep and what needs to go.

Night 19: As the moon decreases in size this is a time for letting go and releasing aspects of self which are no longer needed. This process began in the disseminating moon phase and continues through the last quarter. The following affirmations will assist and guide you through the process of releasing and accepting who you are:

Release

I release you
To soar free
And discover your path

I release you
To go within
And touch your inner child

I release you
To peel away the layers
And find your true self

I release you
To move on and away
From society's expectations

Each night you meditate, take the time to relax, be comfortable, and prepare yourself as described in the For Beginners section.

With a naked face (or even a naked body), stand in front of a mirror and see yourself reflecting back. Don't critique your face or body but look at all of you. Then stare into your own eyes. Try to lose yourself in your own eyes.

Repeat the general statements here or create specific ones for yourself. As you say the statements, visualize each thing leaving your body. This can assist in removing any issues with your inner self. It can also make you more comfortable with your own body and just being in your own skin.

When you meditate it is very important to bring your center back to your physical being. Ground yourself in one of the ways suggested in the For Beginners section.

Night 20: As the moon fades, you rid yourself of unnecessary habits and beliefs. You reach a new understanding of yourself. This is a continued time of harvest. You pluck the foods needed to help you grow and leave behind the chaff that holds you back.

The following chant helps you connect with the universal connection as you harvest and release:

Celestial Guidance

I am a comet streaking across the heavens
Pointing to a path not many will take
I am a meteor falling fast and hot to the earth
Sometimes burning up before I reach my goal
I am a star shining down
Giving guidance towards a dream
I am the moon waxing and waning
Illuminating the inner paths
I am the heavens watching over the earth
Providing security to those in need

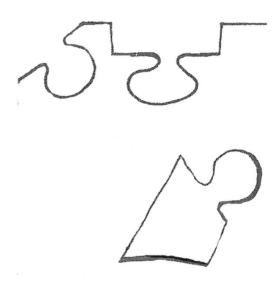

Each night you meditate, take the time to relax, be comfortable, and prepare yourself as described in the For Beginners section.

Look up at the night sky. How does it make you feel? Do you feel small and insignificant, lost in the vastness of the heavens? Do you feel connected to each celestial body?

Pick out one star. Stare at the star until it is the only thing you see in the night sky. Become the star. See how you fit in the cosmic puzzle.

Become yourself again and see how you fit in your own puzzle. Feel the connections both within self and in the universe.

When you meditate it is very important to bring your center back to your physical being. Ground yourself in one of the ways suggested in the For Beginners section.

Night 21: With the waning moon, the night sky is darker. The harvest nears an end and solitude is needed.

Walls

Walls everywhere around me
I can feel them surrounding and protecting
But do they really?
They reflect all that I put out
Echoing back my doubts and fears
I built them carefully and knowingly
Not realizing I was my own prisoner
Stuck behind the confines of this stockade
Echoes from my past reverberate through my mind
Reminding me of old errors and flaws
Like mirrors each section magnifies every mistake
Stop! I scold, Just stop!
Turning slowly I search for any opening
There on my shoulder stands an old friend
A reminder of my inner strength and of lessons learned
She flames the reflections, melting years of pain
Cuing me to praise myself and follow my path
A swipe of her tail cracks the self made barriers
A wave of hope rolls out from me
Widening the crevices and tumbling chunks
Each step forward allows me to topple
More qualms and doubts both old and new
To let compassion and hope shine from me
And reflect back while breaking down
The walls of my prison

Each night you meditate, take the time to relax, be comfortable, and prepare yourself as described in the For Beginners section.

Visualize yourself standing in a room of brick. There are no windows or doors. There is no need to panic – this is your secret hiding place where you are safe.

Look at each brick; see a symbol or word etched in each brick. Feel the rough surface beneath your fingers. This wall is something you built to protect yourself. But as usually happens some of the protections are no longer needed.

As you look at the symbols and words pull out the bricks which are no longer necessary. Shed the habits and instinctive reactions which no longer serve a purpose in your life. You may find only one or two bricks to discard or there may be many. As you touch a brick you no longer need, see it crumble into dust. Shining through the holes you create, see the waning moon bright against the dark sky. Take your time and carefully consider what to discard and what to keep.

When you are done with this visualization, drink some water. It will help wash away the residue from the exercise. Allow yourself time again to breath and recover from the losses you have experienced. Remember the light shining through from the moon is your guidance to a better life. Take time after this to ground and come back to yourself.

When you meditate it is very important to bring your center back to your physical being. Ground yourself in one of the ways suggested in the For Beginners section.

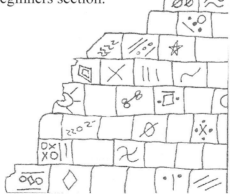

61

Chapter 8: Balsamic Moon

Balsamic moon is less than half illuminated. Her face turns away to hide. This phase allows you to accept the changes you have made. The fading light is like the fading consciousness just before you fall asleep. It is healing and calming.

The comfortable quilt of life covers you once more. You use the darkening night and lack of light as a time to recover and accept.

The night is darker and deeper than before allowing you to rest and mend more completely. The light is dimmer but still it is strong enough to restore your energy as you release the negative aspects of your life. This is the time for you to rebuild your image of yourself.

These meditations help in the healing process after letting go. They help you focus on you and not on all the external noise in your life.

Night 22: Through inner work you have realized how you want to change. Clearing out the old to make room for the new is the focus of this moon phase.

Turning Wheel

With the turning of the wheel
I change
In spring, I am born
Fresh and young, planting seeds for the coming season
In summer, I come to maturity
Tending the seedlings to grow strong and tall
In fall, I harvest the fruits of my labor
Preserving what is needed and composting the rest
In winter, I go to rest to be reborn again
Mulling over what will be needed for the future

With the turning of the wheel
I change
At the waxing of the moon I learn and grow
Considering all options
At the full moon I take in and send out positive energy
Since my healing energy is at a peak
At the waning moon I remix my beliefs to be reborn again
With the turning of the wheel
I change

Each night you meditate, take the time to relax, be comfortable, and prepare yourself as described in the For Beginners section.

See yourself in a meadow during early spring. The ground is still frozen, grass still brown, and trees rattle in the icy breeze.

Now see how nature changes, watch the seasons pass, like you are watching a movie in fast forward. See the grass turn from brown to green. See spring flowers bloom and fade. Feel the temperature rise as the season passes. Watch the green deepen through summer. See the meadow fill with bugs and scents from the growing plants. Feel the crisp cool fall breeze whisper past you. As the scene scurries past, see the grass fade and the trees bordering the meadow burst into flame colored leaves. Watch as squirrels hurry to store away food for the winter. See the first snowfall and the deer leaving tracks. Feel the icy cold flakes fall upon your cheeks. Watch as nature goes through her cycles.

Think about the cycles you've gone through and how you grew and changed through the seasons.

When you meditate it is very important to bring your center back to your physical being. Ground yourself in one of the ways suggested in the For Beginners section.

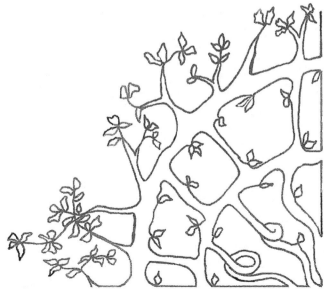

Night 23: The cycle of the moon is drawing near its conclusion. Prepare for an ending and a passing of the moon's energy and a release for your own.

Composting

I pull the veil over me
To go within and recreate
Who I am and what direction I take

I turn the compost of my inner self
Harvesting the new soil
And burying the bits which still need time

I tumble like a stone in a waterfall
Polishing my core beliefs
On this internal journey

Each night you meditate, take the time to relax, be comfortable, and prepare yourself as described in the For Beginners section.

If you have a compost pile, think of these things the next time you turn the pile. If not, visualize yourself turning a compost pile. See the bits of yard and food waste. Dig in your pitch fork and pull up the first forkful. See how water, sun and time have started to break down and change the material. Think about how a particular belief of yours has changed over time. Consider a belief you hold and how that belief may change and grow.

Continue turning the pile. There is an unpleasant odor and perhaps your pile is steaming a bit from all the changes occurring. Smell the rotten food and waste. Change often makes us uncomfortable and creates a break down in key components of who we are.

Dig deeper and see the rich soil at the bottom of the pile. This is the result of Mother Nature's hard work. This soil is the place where she will plant her seeds.

What parts of you do you want to recreate? As you work on yourself you will have bits which need work and others which will be your foundation. See how the soil from the compost nourishes seeds for growth; see how your inner foundation can nourish your own growth.

When you meditate it is very important to bring your center back to your physical being. Ground yourself in one of the ways suggested in the For Beginners section.

Night 24: The light fades with only a sliver left. It is a restful time as you let the energy drain from you

The following chant is meant to give you a feeling of comfort and security:

Cocoon

In my cocoon I sleep
Changes and growth happen
While I rest quiet
Wrapped in a dark veil

In my cocoon I sleep
Transforming and maturing
As the time slips by
And the moon fades to dark

In my cocoon I sleep
Waiting for the time
When I burst forth
Beautifully transformed

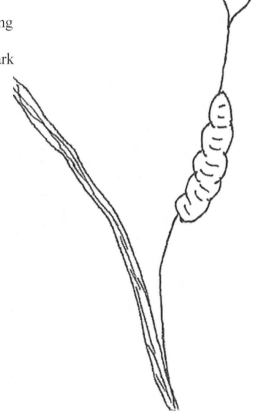

Each night you meditate, take the time to relax, be comfortable, and prepare yourself as described in the For Beginners section.

Curl in a blanket; cover yourself like you are in a cocoon. What about you do you want to shed when you are released from this cocoon? What do you want to make stronger?

Feel the warmth and safety of the cocoon. Change can be scary but if done willingly change will transform you. See yourself as a caterpillar snug in a cocoon. The cocoon is a warm place of safety to mull over all the changes you have wrought. Feel the growth in you, see the wings growing.

When ready, break out of the cocoon to see your beautiful transformation.

When you meditate it is very important to bring your center back to your physical being. Ground yourself in one of the ways suggested in the For Beginners section.

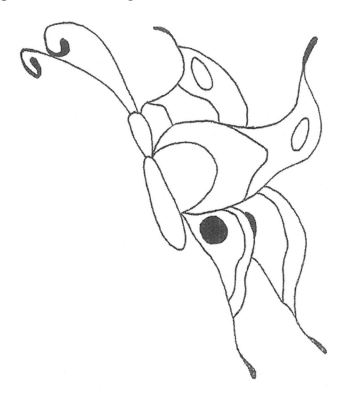

Chapter 9: Dark Moon

Dark moon is the time for remixing all your inner elements in order to move towards rebirth. The face of the moon is hidden from the world just as your focus should be on your inner workings.

The dark moon gives you the cover of darkness to soothe. It offers solitude and a time of stillness to think about all you have been through. It gives you the opportunity to look at all the choices you have, even if some of them seem out of reach. It is a time to consider what you will put into you.

This phase is full of possibilities. You can select any ingredient to include in your life and each one will affect it just a bit differently.

No decisions are made here. It is all about looking at the alternatives available to you.

Night 25: When alone in the dark, use this time for internal consideration. It is when you look at all the components you have been working with and stir them up to help make a better you.

Cauldron of Life

The veil shrouds my face
My light has dimmed behind this mask
The person I was, is no more
Behind my dark curtain I look within
I heal hurts and mend injuries
Whether old or new
I gather construction and creative forces
To prepare for my rebirth
Mixing and stirring the cosmic cauldron
Patiently I wait in excited anticipation
Of what will be born
From the cauldron of life.

Each night you meditate, take the time to relax, be comfortable, and prepare yourself as described in the For Beginners section.

Gather a cauldron or large bowl, symbols of whom you are or who you want to be and something to stir the mixture with. Create a tent (if possible around your cauldron and self. Pick up your first ingredient. This may be pieces of papers with words written on them or pictures from magazines. You can also use actual items to symbolize the components of yourself. Look at this ingredient and acknowledge what it represents. Take some time with each ingredient and really think about how this is part of you and how you want to incorporate this in your life.

Add some or all of it to your cauldron. If you want less of some aspect in your life, then don't add as much. You might also choose to leave out the ingredient if you no longer want it to be part of you. Take your time with each ingredient. Stir after adding each ingredient.

When you are through, leave your cauldron to stew till the new moon.

When you meditate it is very important to bring your center back to your physical being. Ground yourself in one of the ways suggested in the For Beginners section.

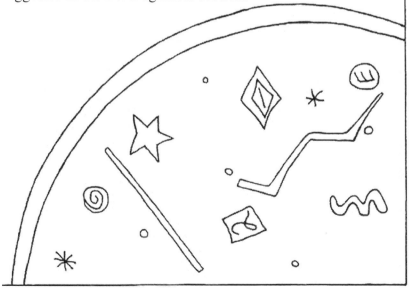

Night 26: The dark moon offers no illumination; you look within yourself to find the universal connection. It is a time to gather your energy and your power.

Cosmic Cauldron

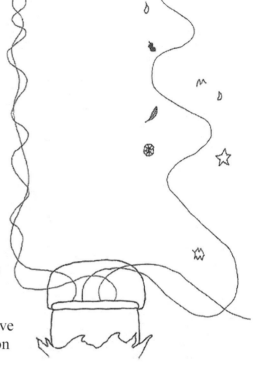

A bit of star dust
A flicker of a moon beam
A flash of sun ray
A touch of celestial charm
Gathered for the stew

A summer breeze
An autumnal leaf
A winter's snowflake
A spring shower
Simmer in the pot

A feather blown on the breeze
A fire warming the hearth
A waterfall crashing down
A stone from deep within a cave
Mixed into the cosmic cauldron

To cook and mesh into something new
Bubbling as it simmers on a mystical fire
Churning and mixing to create life
All in preparation for the impending rebirth

Each night you meditate, take the time to relax, be comfortable, and prepare yourself as described in the For Beginners section.

Take a bit of this animal or plant. Corral a zephyr or a mountain stream to go in your bag. Wander the world collecting your samples, harvest a bit of human emotions and expressions.

Once your bag is full and you have all your samples, stand on the dark moon whose face is hidden. There in the center of a round crater stands a cauldron on a tri-pod. As you approach, a fire starts beneath it. Water fills the cauldron as you open your bag. The only light comes from the fire, everything else is dark.

One by one you add your bits occasionally stopping to stir the magical mixture. You laugh, cry, and sing as you perform your task.

After your last ingredient goes in you stir the cauldron. Close your eyes and let the warmth from the fire wash over you as you pour your energy into the jumble of ingredients. Smell the concoction as it simmers

When you have stirred enough, blow out the fire like birthday candles and sprinkle your mixture. As you drop the mixture, see how you've changed it with your divine powers.

When you meditate it is very important to bring your center back to your physical being. Ground yourself in one of the ways suggested in the For Beginners section.

Night 27: The dark moon is a time of ending but it is also a time of preparing for rebirth. The cycle continues with a new moon after nights of darkness.

The following is to help prepare you for the change in moon cycle:

Energy

Energy flows through me
I am empowered to stand firm and strong
In my beliefs and actions

Energy flows through me
I am empowered to feel and control
All of my emotions

Energy flows through me
I am empowered to trust myself
In all things

Each night you meditate, take the time to relax, be comfortable, and prepare yourself as described in the For Beginners section.

See yourself against the dark velvety sky. You are comfortable and peaceful. Every way you turn you see sparkling stars glimmering at you joyfully. Each is an opportunity. Each is a dream you may attain. The power resides in you. Reach out your hand and you will touch your dream.

Watch the night sky; see which dream or star draws you. Feel it vibrate in your hand, feel it resonate through the depths of your soul.

What is this dream? How can you make it real? Hold it in your heart and take time to cherish it before you release it again.

Repeat this with more than one star or dream. All the stars represent all the possibilities in your life if you are willing to see and embrace them.

Come to Earth gently. Ground after this by lying on the floor or ground. Consider which dream you were drawn to the most. Think about the changes you need to make. What is the first step to give birth to this dream?

When you meditate it is very important to bring your center back to your physical being. Ground yourself in one of the ways suggested in the For Beginners section.

Night 28: Because the moon cycles through each phase at three plus days I opted to put this generic affirmation and meditation at the end of the book. Fit it in when it feels best to you.

Possibilities

I am the earth
Nurturing all the creatures
I am the streams
Bringing change and chaos
I am the wind
Tousling and twisting
I am the fire
Of passion within
I am torn down
Only to be remade better than before
I am nothing
But not lost or forgotten
I am everything
With all the possibilities
I am

Each night you meditate, take the time to relax, be comfortable, and prepare yourself as described in the For Beginners section.

In a dark room, sit quietly with your eyes closed. Breathe deeply and relax your mind and body. As you breathe in, take in all the things from your day, demands from family, work, and friends. As you breathe out, let it go. Shed the stress and strain from the day. Try to empty your mind.

As your mind relaxes, see yourself standing in the dark alone. Slowly turn around. Note any symbols or any words which may appear. Listen for sounds. Pay attention to any textures you feel or flavors you taste. Be in the moment with all your senses. Keep breathing and looking around. You may be left in the dark or you may get indications to follow a path. Follow what happens. See what the divine has to share.

When you meditate it is very important to bring your center back to your physical being. Ground yourself in one of the ways suggested in the For Beginners section.

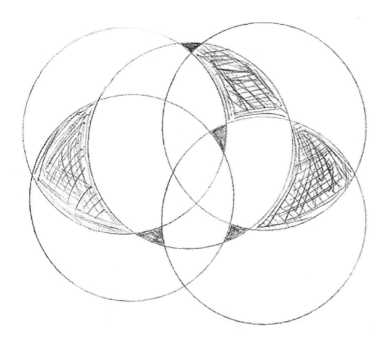

Resources:

All the information for this book came from personal experience and the following resources:

Web Sources:
http://www.themysticeye.com/info/moonphases.htm
http://www.moonconnection.com/moon_phases.phtml

http://www.usno.navy.mil/USNO/astronomical-applications/astronomical-information-center/phases-percent-moon

Book Sources:
Mayall, R Newton; Margaret Mayall; and Jerome Wyckoff, The Sky Observer's Guide, Golden Guides, 1985.

Dickinson, Terence, The Universe and Beyond, Third Edition, Firefly Book, 1999.

Dickinson, Terence, Nightwatch, Third Edition, Firefly Book, 1999.

Levy, David, A Guide to Skywatching, Fog City Press, 2002.

Engelbert, Phillis; Diane L Dupuis, The Handy Answer Book, Visible Ink Press, 1998.

###

About the Author:
From poetry to novel, Eileen enjoys telling a good story or expressing a heartfelt emotion. She's been published in Circle Magazine, The American Tarot Association's Quarterly Journal, What's Cooking America, Children, Churches and Daddies, placed second in Words of Women 2010 Writing Contest, 2012 Daily Flash, and The Deadman's Tome. She has a bachelor's degree in business and a second bachelor's degree in English Professional Writing and Book Editing. On the side, she has a small editing business. In addition to her work, she loves to read, crochet, crafting, research genealogy, and spend time with family. She has three adult daughters and has been married to my husband for over 30 years.

Connect with Eileen at:
blog: http://www.dragonsden64.blogspot.com/
website: http://eileentroemel.weebly.com/
Twitter: https://twitter.com/EileenTroemel
Favorite me on Smashwords:
https://www.smashwords.com/profile/view/kevvs229

Smashwords Interview at:
https://www.smashwords.com/interview/kevvs229

Other books by Eileen:
Secret Past

A romance novel: Waiting in line at the bank, Nick and Dee are thrown together during a bank robbery. Instantly attracted Dee can't resist family-oriented Nick. Dee has secrets – deadly secrets which private eye Nick stirs up. He must know all her secrets. To survive Dee must run but can't leave Nick. Nick escapes with her. Nick has to earn her trust as Dee realizes she is strong enough to face her Secret Past.

About the Artist:
TJ Jahns is a student of art and history. She has taken classes at the Milwaukee Museum of Art, UW Oshkosh and now attends Alverno College. As an amateur artist she does commission work for family and friends. As an amateur historian she finds absolutely everything interesting. As an amateur writer she blogs. She likes animation, video games, nature, music, mystery, pizza and a good story.

Made in the USA
Charleston, SC
01 July 2014